The Highway Turtles

Story by Corinne Fenton

Illustrations by Jenny Mountstephen

Amy and Grace had been fishing
with their grandfather many times.
They always went to his favorite place,
not far from the center of the city.
It had a creek and some ponds
where many kinds of small animals lived.

Every time the twins went there,
they saw ducks swimming on the ponds
and herons standing in the shallows.
They heard frogs croaking
from somewhere in the reeds.

One day, Amy noticed something different in one of the ponds.

"Papa!" she cried.
"There are two brown turtles living here."

A few weeks later,
when they went back to the creek
they saw a large sign with a map on it.

"A highway is going to be built here,"
said Grace. "Right by our fishing spot."

"What will happen to the animals and birds?"
asked Amy. "Won't they be frightened away?"

HIGHWAY

Wetlands Area

Ponds

Creek

Footbridge

Ponds

Wetlands Area

"This will be a wetlands area,"
replied Papa, reading from the sign.
"It will still be a home for the wildlife."

He pointed at the map.
"You can see where the highway
is going to be built beside the creek
and the ponds," he explained.
"There's a very good chance
that the wildlife will stay here
for a long time."

"Oh, good," said Amy.
"Now let's go and look for our turtles
before it gets dark."

As the girls walked toward the pond,
they saw one of the turtles
moving slowly up the bank,
not far from where they were standing.

"Where's it going, Papa?" asked Grace.

"She could be going to lay some eggs,"
answered Papa.

They kept very still and quiet
and watched the turtle.

First of all, she dug a hole in the bank
with her back legs.
Then she laid some eggs
and covered them with sand.

Papa said to the girls,
"Those eggs will hatch
in about two months.
We'll look at the nest
whenever we come here."

The next time they went fishing,
the girls heard the rumble
of big machines approaching.

Huge bulldozers and a digger
were being brought onto the site.

"Oh, Papa," cried Amy.
"They're going to start
building the highway.
I hope the turtle eggs will be safe."

"We'll check the map on our way back,"
said Papa.

The girls found the turtle pond on the map.

"It's all right," said Papa.
"The nest is a long way
from where the machines will be working."

One afternoon, they stayed later than usual.
As the girls went back
across the footbridge with Papa,
they looked down
at the creek and the ponds.
Work had finished for the day
on the highway site,
and the big machines were silent.

Suddenly Amy gasped.
"Look!" she cried. "There's a fox!"

A fox was sneaking out of the bushes
quite close to the turtle's nest.
His eyes were fixed on the pond.
Somehow, the fox sensed
that they were watching
and in a flash, he disappeared.

"Papa, that fox looked hungry," said Grace.
"Will the turtle eggs be all right?"

"We'll just have to hope
that he doesn't find the eggs," said Papa.

All that week, Grace and Amy felt anxious.
They kept thinking about the fox.
Would he discover the turtle eggs?

On their next visit,
the twins ran ahead of Papa.
They went straight to the turtle's nest.
It **had** been disturbed.
There were broken eggshells
and some little holes in the sand
where the nest had been.

Grace and Amy were horrified!

"The fox did find the eggs!" cried Grace.
They stared at the empty nest.

When Papa arrived, he stopped to look
at the edge of the pond.
The twins crouched down beside him.

Suddenly Amy pointed.
"Look at those tiny turtles
in the water," she cried in excitement.
"They must have hatched out of the eggs!"

"So the fox didn't eat them after all!"
said Grace.
"But how did they get into the pond?"

"Baby turtles always find their way
to water by themselves," smiled Papa.

15

The highway was soon finished,
and although there was some traffic noise,
the wildlife stayed in the wetlands.

Grace and Amy went back there many times
with Papa, and the turtle pond
was always their favorite place.